CW00485424

MY FRIEND ANNE FRANK

MY FRIEND ANNE FRANK

Jacqueline (Jopie) van Maarsen

Translated from the Dutch
by Debra F. Onkenhout

VANTAGE PRESS
New York

Published by Vantage Press, Inc.
516 West 34th Street, New York, New York 10001

Manufactured in the United States of America
ISBN: 0-533-12013-6

Library of Congress Catalog Card No.: 96-90350

0 9 8 7 6 5 4

Contents

Preface

Some of my discoveries and remarks concerning Anne and her diary, which are described in this book, have been used by others without mentioning the source. This is, among other things, the case with my answer to the question: Who is Kitty to whom Anne addressed herself in the diary?

MY FRIEND ANNE FRANK

May 1986

Dawn was breaking when I closed the big blue book. I had read all night. I walked to the window. No soldiers shouting commands. A quiet street. High in the sky a sea gull was flying.

Jacque used to say to me, "You're scared to do anything because it may be forbidden." (July 1942)

I went to the kitchen to make a cup of tea and gazed at the abundance of supplies I found in the pantry.

½ lb. tea costs 350 florins. (May 6, 1944)

With a cup of tea in hand I walked over to the bookcase. I took out a book: *Het Achterhuis*.* Cardboard binding, old yellowed paper. The kind of paper still used two years after the war. A card was pasted inside at the beginning: "Otto H. Frank—with kind regards!" Mr. Frank had brought it to me in 1947. It was the first edition of Anne's diary, which he had struggled to get published. I had finished that in one sitting, too.

And now it struck me again that Anne's passion and zest for life, so familiar to me back then, echoed through and through to the very last pages of the book. Even her belief in the goodness of people and in a better world hadn't disappeared during the years she spent shut away behind the nailed-down curtains. I had shared her belief then.

Anne's father died in 1980. He bequeathed all of Anne's original writings to the Dutch state, which then relegated them

*The Dutch version of Anne's diary, translated into English and published under the title *The Diary of a Young Girl*.

1

to the Netherlands State Institute for War Documentation (RIOD). A few months later a notice appeared in the newspaper that the institute intended to publish the complete writings of Anne Frank. I was already familiar with some of her writings. Mr. Frank had let me read them many years after the war. I knew that Anne had written about her classmates, about her girl-friends. It wasn't always exactly flattering. Mr. Frank said to me then, "Who would have ever thought that of our Anne?," referring to the thoughts that she had put into words in her diary.

The thought that one particular passage in her diary would be published strongly displeased me. Her father had not let me read that passage then, but I came across it in the English version. My name was not mentioned in *The Diary of a Young Girl,* but I knew that it was about me because I remembered the incident. I couldn't understand why it was so necessary to disclose all of those intimate details. I wrote a letter to the institute stating my objection to its publication.

I was aware that there were doubts on the part of neo-Nazis about the authenticity of Anne's writings. The Dutch version of her diary published in 1947, *Het Achterhuis*, did not contain all of Anne's notes. For various reasons, her writings were not published in their entirety. Furthermore, Anne had begun re-writing her diary but had not finished it when she was arrested in 1944.

This created some confusion. Through the years the neo-Nazis attacked the authenticity of the diary. It was, after all, proof of the Holocaust. Mr. Frank had been involved in several lawsuits over it.

Then I read in the newspaper that the institute was going to have the handwriting investigated by a handwriting expert and the paper and ink type analyzed. A scientific publication would prove the authenticity of Anne's diary. Completeness of the writings would, therefore, be of utmost importance.

I cast aside my objections. I had always been pleased with

Anne's decision to change not only my last, but also my first name when she started rewriting her diary with the intention of having it published after the war. After a great deal of hesitation, I finally agreed to allow my maiden name, which *had* been mentioned in the original diary, to be mentioned for the sake of authenticity in the publication titled *The Diary of Anne Frank: The Critical Edition*. I loaned certain documents containing Anne's handwriting to the institute. A postcard that was important to the investigation because of its postmark remained in their possession for a number of years.

The institute intended to have *The Diary of Anne Frank: The Critical Edition* ready by 1982. It was 1986 before it was completed.

I started reading it immediately. I was reminded again of how honest Anne was about herself and others. Her honesty had been one of the building blocks of our friendship.

When the war was over I preferred not to think about the difficult war years, but because of Anne's diary I was continually confronted with them. In fact, the more important the diary became, the more I was confronted with those days. The diary has lived with me throughout the years.

And now, as I read Anne's complete writings, the images of those days, engraved in my memory, returned clearly and distinctly to my mind.

March 1943

"You'll all be gassed! You mustn't go; you must go into hiding,"
I heard my mother say. My uncle began shouting at once. Yeah,
yeah, that French sister-in-law of his. She had to say something
sensational again. They had been ordered to appear at the
Hollandse Schouwburg, a playhouse that was the meeting point
from which deportations to Westerbork were organized. They
had decided to go because if they went into hiding and were
found, they would receive an *S** on their identification cards.
And that meant something much worse than just working in a
German concentration camp. An *S* classification meant receiving
almost nothing to eat and working until collapse. *No, it is better
just to go,* my uncle thought.

I had run as fast as my legs would carry me to Tugelaweg.
When I entered the house, my uncle was busy burning cigarette
holes in all of the furniture. No way the Krauts were going to get
any enjoyment out of his furniture. I didn't understand the
meaning of the word *gassing.* It vaguely reminded me of vermin.
I walked toward my youngest cousin, Meta. We no longer
listened to the arguing adults. With our arms around each other
we stood looking at the burn holes in the furniture. *What a
shame,* we thought.

They had been forced by the Germans to move from The
Hague to Amsterdam, and I was glad that we had been able to
play together so much the last couple of months. Meta's older
sisters were already gone, one with her husband and baby and
the other not long afterward with her husband, whom she had
quickly married when she received her summons so that they

---

*An *S* stood for *Straf,* the German word for punishment.

4

could be deported together. On Sinterklaasavond* the younger girls had written a comforting poem for their parents. In it was written: "Although they are far away, God will watch over them." Now their backpacks stood waiting for them, too. They were to leave that evening. My father wept as he embraced his sister. I ran out the door.

On the way home I realized sadly that I had lost yet another playmate. No, there was no need for Anne to be jealous of my running around with someone else now that she was in Switzerland. Ilse had been gone for a long time, too. I had no friends yet at the new school.

After the Christmas holidays I had transferred from Jewish High School to Girls High School. It was if I had arrived from another planet. The Germans had concentrated all of the Jews in one certain section of the city, and apparently the removal of a complete population could go completely unnoticed by those who did not want to see it. The anti-Jewish laws with which I had been confronted over the past two years had left me with an inferiority complex, and I had trouble adjusting. I promptly failed that year and started school again in another class in which I felt more comfortable and made several new friends. I didn't talk about what had taken place in my neighborhood the previous two years and would not talk about it again for many years. That had a lot to do with Anne, my friend, who would later become *Anne Frank*.

*December 5, the evening before Saint Nicholas Day and an important Dutch holiday, especially for children, who receive gifts from Saint Nicholas. It is also customary for older children and adults to write rhymes for each other and exchange small gifts with family and friends.

October 1941

"Jackie, Jacqueline!" I heard being called out behind me. I was bicycling home after my first day of high school. I looked around. A small wisp of a girl with shiny black hair and sharp facial features came bicycling alongside of me out of breath. "Are you going that way, too?" she asked and pointed toward the Berlagebrug. When I nodded yes, she said in a decisive tone, "Then we can bicycle home together from now on. I live at Merwedeplein." And so it happened.

She was in my class at school. I hadn't noticed her there that morning and had to ask her name. "Anne Frank," she said. She took me home with her, introduced me at once to her mother and sister as her new school friend, and went to feed her black cat, already circling her, mewing and rubbing its head against her. Then her grandmother, who lived with them, had to meet me, and I met Anne's father that day, too, because Anne said after an hour, when I wanted to call home, "Just say you'll be staying for dinner." Anne talked endlessly, telling me all about her girlfriends and her previous school, and wanted to know everything about me. Both of us had attended a Montessori school—she the Sixth Montessori on Niersstraat (now known as the Anne Frank School) and I the First Montessori on Corellistraat.

It was very cozy and pleasant at Anne's house, and I felt immediately at home. Her assertiveness and the way in which she had initiated our friendship appealed to me.

When Mr. Frank returned home later, he took the time to talk with me extensively. I told him that I had to go to Jewish High School instead of Girls High School even though I didn't have a Jewish mother and why. He looked at me gravely and said, "I will speak to your parents about that." In light of the later

6

measures my mother took, I gather that he did just that, although I have no knowledge of it.

Since then, I've got to know Jopie de Waal* at the Jewish Secondary School. We are together a lot and she is now my best girl friend. (June 15, 1942—The Diary of a Young Girl)

After a couple of days Anne declared that I was her best friend and that she was mine. I agreed without completely understanding the consequences. It turned out that she could become very angry when I associated with other girls now and then. She considered that a betrayal of our friendship.

*In The Diary of Anne Frank: The Critical Edition (published by RIOD, the Netherlands State Institute for War Documentation). Jacqueline van Maarsen.

1920-1940

My mother had been brought to Amsterdam from Paris by the management of the Hirsch fashion house at the Leidseplein to be in charge of its haute-couture department. She purchased patterns and fabrics in Paris and also did some designing herself. Since Hirsch's clients were members of the upper class and spoke fluent French, as was common in those days, my mother didn't really exert herself to learn Dutch. Therefore, she hadn't gotten much further than "the soldier is brave" and "the sailor is proud" when she met my father. He spoke such excellent French that my mother fell in love with him before realizing that he was Dutch. She fled back to Paris; she had no intention of remaining in Holland the rest of her life. She did not mind the fact that he was Jewish. She had already abandoned her Catholic faith one day at age eighteen when the priest began to ask indiscreet questions. On her way home, in tears, she had shouted, *"Le salaud,"* ("dirty old man" in French), and she never set foot in the church again.

My father did not give up easily; he went after her and moved his import-export business to Paris. Before they married, my mother took classes and converted to Judaism. She did not tell her parents; although they were quite taken with their Jewish son-in-law, this would have been more than they could handle.

My sister was born in Paris, but after a year my mother had had enough of playing housewife. My father preferred to continue his business in Holland anyway, and my mother saw the possibility of building up her own haute-couture business in Amsterdam. When they moved back, a second baby announced itself. This did not fit in with my mother's plans, but nevertheless, I was born in January 1929. Because my mother worked during the day there was a nanny for the daily care of her daughters. My father busied himself intensively with our upbringing. He

8

delved into the Montessori teaching method just on the rise and enrolled us in the First Montessori School on Corellistraat. During the thirties the classes there were flooded with children who had fled Nazi Germany with their parents. The Montessori method lent itself better to educating children who were not in command of the local language than a classical education did. The children adjusted well, and particularly the children my age who had already come to Holland in 1933 quickly learned to speak Dutch without an accent.

In 1937 we moved from the Willemsparkweg to the Albrecht Dürerstraat. On the undeveloped land on Cliostraat near our house new houses were being built. When they were finished, a girl moved into one of them. I was playing with a ball, and suddenly she approached me: "Can you play with two balls?" I had already seen her watching but wasn't too responsive myself. I thought it was nice, though, that she spoke to me, and we became friends. One afternoon she went with me to Brownies. Afterward we were going to stop by her grandmother's house there in the neighborhood. Her older sister was there, too. When Bertie said that she wanted to become a Brownie, her sister announced, "I'm going to become a member of the Jeugdstorm."* Her grandmother, her mother's mother, was furious and scolded Bertie's sister terribly. I knew, of course, what the Jeugdstorm was about and knew not to give my opinion in front of Bertie, whom I liked very much. Not long afterward I saw her sister indeed walking with the orange-and-black Jeugdstorm cap, and her brother became a member also. Bertie didn't, but she didn't join the Brownies either, which, by the way, had disbanded, since the war had broken out in the meantime. Her father appeared soon afterward in the black uniform worn by the members of the Dutch Nazi party.

*Nazi youth organization.

In April 1940, after the Germans had invaded Denmark, I made a doll out of clay. I imagined that it had some sort of magical power that would keep the Germans from coming to Holland. On May 10, however, it happened. We heard airplanes flying over at night, and my parents sat listening to the radio early in the morning. Family and friends stopped by all day and talked agitatedly. Every now and then I caught bits and pieces of their conversations, including, "fleeing by boat to England." The air-raid siren went off a couple of times a day, and then we sat in the cellar under the house until the all-clear signal had been given. Everyone glued strips of brown paper to the windows (a preventive measure to hold the window intact in the event that the vibrations from the bombings caused the glass to shatter), and my sister and I hoarded away a shoe box full of candy, which was already empty a month later. After five days Holland capitulated, and the next day we heard that our Jewish baker, who had fled to Holland from Germany several years earlier and came by every day with his cart, had committed suicide together with the rest of his family. We children were excluded from everything to the extent possible, but we felt the frightened tension of the adults. I dumped my clay doll into a nearby canal.

My mother's fashion house went downhill due to the circumstances surrounding the war and would be completely closed down a few months later, since non-Jewish seamstresses were no longer permitted to work for her. Even Rika, the maid who had been with us for years, had to leave.

My father began trading in old books and prints, which he had collected and enjoyed for many years. My parents could foresee that they would soon be unable to pay the high rent on the Albrecht Dürerstraat. A large part of the beautiful antique furniture was sold, and in September we moved to the Hunze-straat; thus my problem with Bertie solved itself.

In February 1941 Jews were required to register. My mother

was not considered Jewish by the Germans, as she had four "Aryan" grandparents. Those who had two Jewish grandparents did have to register but were still excluded from the anti-Jewish laws enacted by the Germans at the beginning of the occupation unless they were members of a Jewish congregation. Such was the case with my sister and me. When my parents returned from Paris, my father had gone to great pains to have his wife acknowledged as a Jew by the Orthodox Jewish congregation in Amsterdam. It wasn't easy, but in 1938 he finally succeeded. My sister and I could then become members of the Jewish congregation, for we now had, according to Jewish law, a Jewish mother.

So it happened that my sister and I were also considered Jewish by the Nazis, and this was the story that I told Mr. Frank the first time I met him.

The Beginning

Before the war I went to the Cineac on Reguliersbreestraat every Sunday morning with my father. I enjoyed *The Kids* and *Popeye* and other cartoons. I couldn't really appreciate the chaotic predicaments in the Laurel and Hardy series or the pie throwing, and seeing and hearing about a certain Adolf Hitler made me come unglued. My father went, without a doubt, to see the world news. He was certainly worried about what was happening in Germany but consoled himself with the fact that it was far away. It was unthinkable to him that the Germans would occupy Holland, and once that happened he and many others could not imagine that it would last so long. I shared his optimism eagerly.

During that time Jewish acquaintances who had fled Germany came to visit us regularly. Sometimes I caught part of the discussions, which did impress upon me how awful everything was that was happening in Germany, but I did not understand exactly what was going on. We weren't told, and I didn't ask. The only thing I read in the newspaper was a comic strip called *Bruintje Beer*. The distance between children and adults was great, and I expected that the chaos created by the adults would also be resolved by them.

I have no personal recollections of anti-Semitism before the war. I didn't experience any of the verbal anti-Semitic abuse that I heard being told about later. My dark features were considered to be related to my French blood, and I have my father's blue eyes.

After the Germans invaded Holland, everything seemed to go on as usual at first. However, at the beginning of 1941 I experienced something I thought was just an incident, but which soon proved itself to be the beginning of the persecution of Jews in Holland.

David

My father had two sisters. The older one lived with her husband and four daughters in The Hague. Their youngest daughter, Meta, was my age. We got along well with each other and stayed with each other frequently during vacations. Deetje was often with us, too; she was the daughter of my father's younger sister and lived in Amsterdam. She was a couple of months younger than I. My father also had three brothers.

We held the Seder, the commemoration of the Jews' exodus from Egypt thousands of years ago in the days of the pharaohs, at Deetje's house every year. Although one is required to stay seated for an awfully long time during the Seder, I always enjoyed it anyway. I sat next to my cousin, and sometimes we chatted secretly. She had Hebrew lessons and could follow along easily. I couldn't read the Hebrew letters written in the book used during the Seder but found it interesting that it had to be read from back to front. I followed the story in Dutch, which was printed next to the Hebrew text, and looked at the illustrations. In one picture there was a man in a long black robe who spread his arms, causing the sea to part. Thus the Jews had free passage, and after they had all crossed the sea, it closed again, just at the moment that their pursuers arrived. In fact, one could see the pursuers' front line floundering in the sea. And so everything worked out for the best again. We were also allowed to drip red wine on the white tablecloth with our pinkies, and at a certain point the door was opened to let the prophet enter. He never came, though. During the Seder we ate my aunt's delicious homemade vegetable soup. At the end of the evening, when we children had almost fallen asleep, songs were sung. Little by little I learned the melodies of the songs, but I couldn't sing them since I couldn't read the Hebrew lyrics.

In later years Deetje's cousin David was there, too. He was

about five years older than we were and attended teacher training college. David was supposed to go to Palestine. After his father died, David started coming to the Seder at my uncle and aunt's house with his mother and sister. From that moment on, he conducted the Seder. In spite of his youth, he had assumed the role of head of the family since his father's death and supported his mother as much as he could. David always joked with us, and we thought he was nice. He came to our house to visit, too, and my mother always served him tea from a crystal glass in a pretty silver holder reserved especially for him. David observed the Jewish dietary laws. The silver holder is now standing in my cupboard—the glass is broken.

One day in the spring of 1941 Deetje came to pick me up at my house. She said that she was going to her aunt's house and asked whether I wanted to come along. I knew that David had already been gone for a while. He had been picked up by the Germans in the neighborhood of Waterlooplein (where many Jews lived back then). His mother had received a short message from him saying that he was on the way to a work camp in Germany but had heard nothing from him since. I don't know whether Deetje knew what was waiting for us at her aunt's house and that was the reason she wanted me with her. I didn't think to ask her at the time. When we went inside, I saw a note lying on the table and in it David's name and the words *deceased* and *Mauthausen*. David's mother lay screaming and crying on the sofa. I remember Deetje going to get a glass of water from the kitchen. I stood there, unable to move, looking at David's mother. I have never forgotten that picture of grief. It has fixed itself in my memory along with so many other images of those days.

This incident took place during my last year at the Montessori school. At the end of that year it appeared that I would be enrolled in Girls High School without having to take an entrance examination.

Segregation

In May 1941 the first unpleasant experiences started for me, too.

I joined a swim club because I wanted to learn to dive. One afternoon while the whole group stood on the side of the swimming pool, the instructor said that she was very sorry, but the Jewish children would no longer be allowed in the pool. A couple of children, including myself, freed themselves from the group and while being stared after by the others (at least, that was how we felt all of our humiliation) slunk away.

On one of the last days of the school year the Jewish students were summoned by the school principal. The graduating students were told that Jewish children were no longer being accepted at the next school they were supposed to attend. While I was standing there after school discussing it with two girls who had been told the same thing, a group of boys came up and shoved us and softly chanted, "Jew-girls, Jew-girls." It frightened us, and we dashed off.

During the summer vacation I made some short bicycle trips around Amsterdam with a girlfriend with whom I would have gone to Girls High School, but when her school started in September I didn't see her anymore. Shortly thereafter came the decree that Jews were no longer allowed to visit non-Jews. We had played together every Wednesday afternoon for six years. Forty-five years later I read:

> Among other things I told him* the incident that had happened to Jacque and about how girls are completely defenseless when faced with such strong boys. (March 23, 1944)

*Peter van Pels.

I had forgotten that I had told Anne about that incident, which had happened a few months before I met her. During one of our bicycle trips Adrie and I had sat down at the foot of a small dike. Adrie went to pick flowers while I sat reading. Suddenly two strapping boys approached me and tried to kiss me. I fended them off and bit them. They were angry: "Dammit!" Adrie came walking up. I can still see her standing at the top of the dike, flowers in her hand, gazing in astonishment at the tumult in which I had gotten mixed up. When they saw that I wasn't alone, the boys quickly disappeared. My dress was open. I fastened the snaps. Adrie and I looked at each other and started laughing uncontrollably. Then we quickly bicycled home.

The story had evidently made an impression on Anne!

Jewish High School still had to be established and would not begin until October. For me, going to high school was quite an event. I got a stack of new books that needed book covers and labels, and I reconciled myself somewhat to the new circumstances. I shut out all of the unpleasant incidents and cheerfully started the new school year, to which my friendship with Anne would add an extra dimension.

Anne

Anne and I shared the same interests. We were both very eager to learn and did our homework together, which really amounted to my helping her with math. While she finished her homework I was usually nearby doing other things, since I never had to do much for math and languages and thought it was nonsense to study geography and history when you could look everything up anyway. As a result I received some "unsatisfactories," while the diligent Anne excelled.

During the winter that followed we had a wonderful time together. We read the same books, one of our favorites being *Joop ter Heul,* by Cissy van Marxveldt.* We never tired of reading scene after scene to each other and constantly laughed about it. I had received *The Myths of Greece and Rome* from my father. Anne particularly liked the illustrations and requested it for her birthday. Because it was a sewn book, she immediately had it bound. I didn't, and my copy is now lying in pieces in a box.

> Amongst other things I was given . . . some money. Now I can buy *The Myths of Greece and Rome*—grand! (June 14, 1942—*The Diary of a Young Girl*)

*Up until the Second World War, Cissy van Marxveldt (1889–1948) was the most popular author of girls' books in Holland. Her biggest success was *The HBS-Times of Joop ter Heul.* With this book she was the first Dutch author to write books about school life that were not boring, solid, and virtuous. A whole series of "Joop ter Heul" books followed. Van Marxveldt was probably inspired by the book *Little Women,* by Louisa May Alcott, published in 1867. In this book family life was described humorously and realistically for the first time. There appear to be many similarities between Joop ter Heul and Jo March in *Little Women.*

We played all kinds of games, our preference being Monopoly. (That, too, is still lying in my cupboard.) Frequently, Anne's sister Margot and my sister, or Sanne and Lies, Anne's friends from elementary school, or new classmates played with us. Anne was always difficult about a girlfriend who had graduated from elementary school with me. She lived quite a long way away, and when we had to hand in our bicycles to the Germans we didn't see each other outside of school much anymore. Later I read, surprised:

> She has got right round Jacque which is a real pity. (June 15, 1942)

Another girl, Ilse, had a Ping-Pong table at home. We often went there to play, and that year we started a Ping-Pong club.

> Susanne Ledermann is our president, Jacqueline van Maarsen the secretary, Elizabeth Goslar, Ilse, and I are the other members. (June 20, 1942)

My movie star collection was much smaller than Anne's—my only idols were Deanne Durbin and Shirley Temple, while Anne also had many UFA* stars—and we spent hours sorting and completing her collection. I collected picture postcards, and Anne enjoyed that as well. We traded cards, and since my collection was larger I also gave her some of my cards that she especially liked.

> Thanks to Daddy, who had brought my film-star collection and picture postcards on beforehand, and with the aid of paste-pot and brush, I have transformed the wall into one gigantic picture. (July 11, 1942—*The Diary of a Young Girl*)

*Universum-Film-Aktiengesellschaft, a German film company.

I knew that Anne loved beautiful clothes and once read a prewar newspaper clipping to her about an evening gown that my mother had made and which was connected to a story. The clipping had been saved together with a note from the customer. (My mother had taken a firm stand on the color of the dress in spite of the customer's protests.) From the *Haagse Post,* dated January 4, 1930: "One of the most striking figures at the Christmas dinner was Mrs. van H.-B. of Aerdenhout, who appeared in an enchanting gown of gold lace which looked magnificent with her strawberry blond hair." All of the other evening dresses were described as well, and we dreamed away about "after the war" when we, too, would appear at balls and parties in "enchanting gowns." Naturally, we patterned ourselves after the heroines in the books by Cissy van Marxveldt.

Meanwhile we contented ourselves with the little parties that Anne staged. She rented movies, and the girls and boys who were in her good graces at the time were invited to her house. I helped her with the planning and the invitations. Such was the case on the Sunday after her thirteenth birthday.

I had my birthday party on Sunday afternoon. We showed a film *The Lighthouse Keeper* with Rin-Tin-Tin, which my school friends thoroughly enjoyed. We had a lovely time. There were lots of girls and boys. (June 15, 1942—*The Diary of a Young Girl*)

Other children also organized those kinds of afternoons. Jewish children were no longer permitted to go to children's films at movie theaters. Later that year, when Anne was already gone, I went to a performance by two Jewish cabaret artists, Johnny & Jones, which only Jews were allowed to attend. Because the Germans regularly raided events where large numbers of Jews congregated, I had a lot of trouble finally getting my parents' permission to go.

When spring came, Anne and I sat out regularly on "the terrace," the flat roof behind the upstairs room at Anne's house, to enjoy the sun. We told each other all kinds of secrets there.

So cut them up into tiny pieces, just like we did that time on the terrace with the note from Mummy's box. (September 25, 1942)

She was extremely curious about sexual relations between men and women and pumped her father constantly for information. He invented all sorts of subterfuge, which she then told me and which really made me laugh, but I was able to enlighten her somewhat, since my sister had already told me the essentials a few years earlier:

That it wasn't the stomach that babies came from is something else I learned from Jacque, who said simply: "The finished product comes out where it went in!" (March 18, 1944)

However, her curiosity was a long way from being satisfied by this tidbit of information, and she kept coming back with other stories she had wormed out of various people and to which she added her own fantasies. At the same time she in turn felt the need to sexually enlighten others, including the youngest boy in the class, with whom she had gone to elementary school. This gave her the feeling of being grown up, which was very important to her. Her sister, Margot, was a couple of years older, and Anne was regarded as a small child who could frequently be very troublesome. She rebelled when she wasn't taken seriously. She came to me once extremely angry after she had been to the dentist on Jan Luykenstraat with her mother and Margot. Margot went on with her mother afterward to do some shopping, but Anne was not allowed to go with them. She was so angry at her mother and jealous of Margot. I thought that Margot and her mother were always very sweet to Anne and patient with her and told her as much, but it didn't help, and she stayed angry.

That summer we often went to a Jewish ice cream parlor called Oasis, not far from home, where only Jews were allowed. We always ran into people we knew there. Anne loved walking behind boys and fantasizing that they were all her admirers. I didn't notice too much admiring going on, but they probably found her amusing, since she was cheerful and lively. Once in a while she would go for a walk with one of the boys. I teased her about him.

My girl friend Jacque teases me the whole time about Hello. (July 3, 1942)

I knew full well that she was only flirting and that it wasn't anything serious. She wanted to experience everything.

Although we had totally different personalities, we stayed best friends, and Anne continued to stress that verbally as well as in writing. When I got my autograph book back from her after she had written a poem for me in it, I was moved by the personal little twist she had given to an otherwise often used verse:

Amsterdam, March 23, 1942

Dear Jackie,
Always show your sunny side,
And be a nice girl at school;
Remain my dearest little friend,
And everyone will love you.

In remembrance of your friend,
Anne Frank

In her farewell letter to me she would write:

P.S. I hope that we'll always stay *"best"** friends until we meet again. (September 25, 1942)

She really didn't accept my going to another friend's house, but gradually there came a time when I would disobey Anne's imperative instructions by seeing Ilse, too, once in a while. This happened a couple of weeks before Anne was to disappear from my life forever, but we didn't know that then.

Jacque is now suddenly very chummy with Ilse and is acting childish and silly toward me. (June 19, 1942)

"She was simply jealous," her father said to me when, to my surprise, I saw this passage and others like it in Anne's original diary, which he let me read almost thirty years later. He had kept these remarks made by his daughter hidden from me and had also deemed them unsuitable for publication when he prepared the manuscript for the first printing of *Het Achterhuis*. I acknowledged his words but didn't elaborate.

Anne also didn't understand that I didn't always need to have people around and sometimes just wanted to read or draw alone. She always had to have someone around to talk to or play with or else she became bored.

Jopie slept here on Saturday night, but she went to Lies on Sunday and I was bored stiff. (June 30, 1942—*The Diary of a Young Girl*)

Though we were together often, we almost never went to school together because I always ran late and preferred not to

*Quotation marks and underlining by Anne.

agree to come by and pick her up. The rest of the day, however, we were inseparable.

Anne constantly wanted me to spend the night at her house or else invited herself to mine. The day before my birthday she also wanted to spend the night. That way she could be the first one to wish me a happy birthday and give me a present. She normally brought along a suitcase containing everything needed for a slumber party as well as a cosmetic case with her curlers, hairbrush, and cape. She made everything fun. I have never met anyone else since then who enjoyed life as completely as my friend Anne did.

I basked in the warmth of her affection and gave her as much of myself as I possibly could. At times that was difficult, because I was the reserved type and was sometimes at my wits' end with her uninhibited declarations of friendship and excessive zeal. At one of our "sleepovers" she embarrassed me terribly. She wrote about it herself:

I asked Jacque whether as proof of our friendship we might feel one another's breasts. Jacque refused. (January 5, 1944)

She didn't like the fact that I wouldn't go along with her proposal, but when I let her give me a kiss on the cheek she was satisfied again, though I found even that to be excessive. Above all, it was her curiosity I wanted to temper. She found breasts extremely interesting, wore one of Margot's bras stuffed with cotton, and had discovered that I did not need to resort to such devices.

Yet this incident did relieve the tension in our friendship. In my own way I had let her know what my limits were, and at that point I also told her that she had to give me a bit more freedom. She was going for walks with Hello, wasn't she?

All the same, I knew very well, and in all honesty I must confess after so many years, that I didn't need to be afraid of

24

competition from Hello, whereas everybody was terribly fond of Ilse, including Anne. Ilse was a sweet and sensible girl. (She died on April 2, 1943, in Sobibor.)

Further on in her diary Anne also writes:

> "At the moment she [Jacque] is being very nice again and I hope it stays like that. I now think quite differently about the things I wrote down earlier."

Because I was often at the Franks' house it struck me one day that all of the chairs had disappeared from the living room and that there were different chairs around the table. I mentioned it and the reply was, "They've been sent away to be reupholstered." I did not understand. Didn't these people have anything better to worry about than a couple of chairs that might be showing signs of wear and tear? If the truth be known, I had always thought the chairs looked nice, but I kept my mouth shut.

I talked to Anne later about my puzzlement. I had started to feel a great threat emanating from the German soldiers who now controlled the city scene in Amsterdam. During the school year it was decreed that all Jews must wear a yellow Star of David* prominently displayed on their clothing. We thereby became instantly recognizable and at the same time completely vulnerable. With the star it was easier to verify whether we were in compliance with the long list of regulations decreed by the Germans. Not only Germans, but also "NSBers" (Dutch Nazis), as well as people who would inform on Jews for a couple of guilders, could be dangerous. By accident, I had already sat on a bench in the square after that was no longer allowed and almost walked into a store no longer open to Jews. One could be picked up for such offenses.

*A six-pointed star and a symbol of Judaism.

Jopie used to say to me, "I'm scared to do anything, because it may be forbidden." (June 20, 1942—*The Diary of a Young Girl*)

Suddenly several children were absent from class. The roundups had started in the Jewish neighborhoods, and one never knew who had "gone into hiding" and who had been "taken away." All at once these two phrases took on new meanings. The boy who had been enlightened by Anne was the first to be absent: in hiding? Many years later I ran into him again. He had indeed gone into hiding. Another one of the first to be absent was Betty, a sweet girl whom Anne described as "fairly quiet."* Again that uncertainty. I never saw her again, and that goes for most of the children in that class, including Ilse. In April 1942 she had written the words "a long, happy life" in my autograph album.

On Monday, July 6, Lies came to me and told me that the Frank family was gone. "Gone to Switzerland!" she added excitedly. Her parents had heard that from the Franks' subtenant. He had found a letter that clearly seemed to indicate the trip to Switzerland. The day before, Anne and I had talked for a while on the phone, and there had been no indication that she would disappear the following day:

When you telephoned me on Sunday afternoon I couldn't say anything, for my mother had told me not to, the whole house was upside down and the front door was locked. (September 25, 1942)

I was happy that Anne and her family had been able to get away in time, and that feeling compensated for the sudden

*June 15, 1942.

feeling of emptiness I experienced because my friend had disappeared. I honestly expected to see her again in the very near future. After all, the war could not possibly go on much longer.

We decided to go to Merwedeplein to see if we could find Anne's diary. We were very curious about it. She had gotten it for her birthday, and I knew that she had described all of the girls and boys in the class in it. We wanted to see what she had written about us. The "mysterious letter" from her father never even crossed my mind.

> I've heard meanwhile that Hanneli and Jacque (at least I think it was them) were in our house to look at my diary, they wanted to get hold of Daddy's mysterious letter of course. (August 14, 1942)

We were able to get inside since Mr. Goldsmith, who had rented a room from them, was home. The beds were unmade, and the kitchen had not been tidied. One particular image from that visit to the Frank family's abandoned house has been etched in my memory: Anne's unmade bed and on the floor in front of it her new shoes, as if they had just been kicked off. An unmade bed was totally unlike Anne, and she had been so happy with those shoes and so proud that the soles were made of wood laminate with rubber taps. Our wooden shoes (leather was practically unobtainable anymore) had inflexible soles. I couldn't understand why she hadn't taken them with her but later realized that she would be able to buy real leather shoes in Switzerland.

Aside from her diary, movie star collection, and postcards, it looked as if she had left all of her games and books behind. I saw Variéte, the game that she had just gotten for her birthday and which we had played like crazy the past few weeks, still lying there. I could barely resist the temptation to take it, but didn't. It was forbidden by the Germans to remove anything from a house that had been abandoned by its Jewish inhabitants, and so we left everything alone.

> If no Germans have been to our apartment so far, please could you go round to Mr. Goldsmith and pick up some of our books and papers and games. You can have them or look after them for me, or else you could take them to Mrs. Gies. (September 25, 1942)

I looked around once more to make sure there wasn't a letter for me from Anne lying there somewhere, but I didn't inquire about one. Anne and I had promised to write each other a "farewell letter" if one of us had to leave unexpectedly. I wasn't to receive it until years later.

> This is the promised farewell letter. (September 25, 1942)

1942–43

When we returned to school again after vacation the classes had shrunk considerably. Teachers were gone, too: in hiding or taken away? We had no idea. No one told us and no one asked questions. After the war I heard what had happened to some of the teachers, either through their own writings (Jacques Presser, who became a professor at the University of Amsterdam after the war and wrote a literary standard about the persecution of the Jews) or as described by others (the biology teacher Dr. B. in *Nearer to You* by Gerard Reve, a well-known Dutch author, in which Reve tells of the death of the biology teacher who committed suicide when she received her notice of deportation to Westerbork. She had been Reve's own teacher before being forced by the Germans to teach at a Jewish school). Some of them I encountered again after the war once they had resumed their professions.

I was now seeing a lot of one of the boys in my class. Our parents were friends. They had not considered going into hiding, since his father had an English passport: that appeared to afford the family protection. Since they were the only Jewish friends of ours left, we held the Seder with them that spring of 1943. My boyfriend brought me a blue-and-white beaded bracelet. It was to be the last time that I would ever see him. I thought, *If I take good care of this bracelet he'll come back again.* It is still lying tucked away in a little box, but the boy never came back.

In the meantime there were more and more rumors that the Germans had begun a total genocide, known as the Endlösung der Judenfrage.* The deportation of Jews out of

*The Final Solution, a term applied by Nazis to the genocide of European Jews during the war.

Holland via Westerbork to Germany and Poland was well under way by the end of 1942. In order to accomplish the "total destruction of the Jewish race," the Jews in all German-occupied countries had to be concentrated in one area. They began with hard labor, starvation, torture, and execution, but the concentration camps became overcrowded the more efficiently organized the operation became, and the destruction method did not proceed quickly enough to suit the Germans. The first rumors about gassing and subsequent burning of the bodies to cover the evidence were already being heard. Many people could not believe it, one of them being my father.

In the fall of 1942 Deetje and her parents had been picked up at home during a roundup and deported. My father's youngest brother, who lived in Amsterdam, also disappeared suddenly. I stopped hearing from another brother who lived in Haarlem with his wife. I asked about them, and it turned out that they were already gone, too. My parents hadn't had the heart to tell us about it. I was angry that I hadn't been told. We had spent so many vacations at their house, often with my aunt's other nieces and nephews, during which time we were spoiled to our heart's content. My aunt had no children of her own. She never forgot our birthdays, and her birthday cards are still part of my postcard collection.

My mother recognized that it was about to become a matter of life or death for her children, and she took action. She had seen the writing on the wall and wouldn't allow herself to be lulled to sleep by hopeful optimism. She decided to have my father's actions that had made us Jewish children undone. The minute he found out, my father would have dug his heels in against it; thus he wasn't allowed to know anything about it, and she forbade us to discuss it.

My mother had undergone a kind of transformation. She usually walked around the whole day now in an old bathrobe, as she believed that haute couture was an art form that had no place at the moment. She was not someone who attributed status to beautiful clothes and was not snobbish. Our maids as well as the baronesses my mother counted as her customers respected and admired her. Together with a Jewish apprentice she now made and altered clothing herself. In addition, she did the housecleaning (we were not allowed to help for fear our hands would be ruined), and she also did the cooking for the first time in her life. After all, our maid was gone.

I had complete faith in my mother. I knew that everything would work out fine for us if she took action. My blind faith did not let me down. One day she walked out the door in full glory, perfectly dressed in carefully preserved clothes with a beautiful hat on her head. She went to the *Sicherheitsdienst* (Nazi Security Service) on Euterpestraat. She told them that my father had made us members of the Jewish congregation without her knowledge and that she wanted to have that reversed. She made sure that she got to speak to someone higher up who also spoke French and, with the aid of her iron will and French charm, managed to convince him that he had to help her. Her ruse worked. She was assured that if she could produce the birth certificates and baptismal certificates of her own four grandparents, our membership in the Jewish congregation would be reversed as well as our registration as Jews in the German records.

This was easier said than done. Although my grandparents had lived in Paris (they had both died at the beginning of the war), they had been born in what was now unoccupied France. That was where the documents had to come from, and time was of the essence. My sister was almost sixteen and could, therefore, be ordered to report to a work camp soon.

My mother enlisted the help of her brother in Paris. My uncle, who was extremely concerned about the hornets' nest his sister had gotten herself into, was more than happy to help. He had no children of his own and was crazy about both of his nieces from Amsterdam. We went to Paris almost every year during summer vacation, and right before the war he had proudly toured the World's Fair with us. We were wearing spotless white sailor dresses and white gloves. Together we had looked at all the different pavilions and had taken a boat tour on the Seine.

In order to get hold of the desired documents quickly, my uncle in turn had to call upon one of his uncles, who was married to my grandfather's sister. During the war this great-uncle was the manager of a famous restaurant on the Champs-Elysées in Paris. There he witnessed the comings and goings of high German officers, and he probably wasn't too fond of Jews—I was never told anything more about it—but still he used his influence, and before long the necessary papers lay at Euterpestraat. My sister and I were removed from the deportation list, as well as my father.

At the same time my mother took another measure: her children had to become Catholics as fast as possible. To that end we went to Waterlooplein once a week so that the priest from the Moses and Aaron Church could teach us the catechism. We each received a beautiful gilt-edged, leather-bound book with a ribbon. The only thing I can remember about it is the "white lie." I continued to ponder over where to draw the line and how you were supposed to know when you were allowed to lie and when you were not. I thought of the example of my father asking us where we were going and whether I had to tell him or not. It was a dilemma for me, but he never asked.

In the meantime my father had discovered that my mother had been to Euterpestraat. After muttering his objections, he realized that she intended to forge ahead; and when the Christmas holidays started we were allowed to remove the yellow star from our clothing, and I left Jewish High School. We did not return to the priest, since the church was in the *Judenviertel* (Jewish quarter), where we were no longer allowed. My father

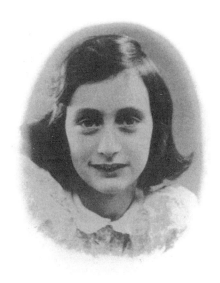

Anne and Jacqueline ("Jopie")

Anne's poem in Jacqueline's autograph album.

20 Lieve Jacqueline,   15 - Sept. 1942.

Ik schrijf je deze brief om afscheid van je te nemen,
dat zal je denkelijk wel verwonderen, maar het
lot heeft het nu een maal niet anders bestemd, ik moet
weg (zoals je inmiddels natuurlijk allang gehoord
hebt) met mijn familie, de reden zal je zelf wel weten.
Toen je me Zondag middag opbelde kon ik je niets
zeggen, want dat mocht niet van moeder, het hele
huis stond toen al op zijn kop en de huisdeur was
afgesloten. Hello zou komen, maar er werd niet

opengedaan. Ik kan niet aan iedereen schrijven
en daarom doe ik het ook alleen maar aan jou. Ik
neem aan dat je niemand over deze brief spreekt
en van wie je hem gekregen hebt, ook niet. Als je zo
vriendelijk wilt zijn met mij geheime corresponden-
tie aan te houden zou ik je daar zeer dankbaar
voor zijn. Inlichtingen mevrouw Gies!!! Ik hoop
dat wij elkaar spoedig zullen zien, maar het zal
vermoedelijk toch niet voor het einde van de
oorlog zijn. Als Lies of iemand anders je ooit vraagt
of je nooit iets van mij hoort zeg dan nooit jawel.
Want je brengt mevrouw Gies en ons in levensge-
vaar, en ik hoop ook dat je zo verstandig bent.
Je mag later natuurlijk wel vertellen dat je een
brief van mij gehad hebt, een afscheid. Welnu Jackie
het ga je goed, ik hoop dat ik gauw een levens-
teken van je ontvang en tot spoedig weerziens.
Je beste vriendin Anne
P.S. Ik hoop dat we elkaar terugzien
altijd beste vriendinnen blijven. dàg.

3   Tweede brief.   25 Sept. 1942.

23 Lieve Jackie,
Je brief heeft me erg verheugd, als er nog niemand van de Duitsers in onze woning geweest
is, kan je wel naar mijnheer Goldschmidt gaan
en wat boeken en schriften en spulletjes van
ons weghalen je mag te houden of voor me
bewaren, maar je kunt ze ook naar mevrouw
Gies brengen. Ik heb je in mijn vorige brief vergeten
te zeggen, dat je deze brieven niet mag bewaren,
want niemand mag ze vinden. Snipper ze dus in

zulke kleine stukjes als wij toen op het plat met het
briefje uit het doosje van moeder gedaan hebben.
Ik hoop dat je het doet. Hoogacht het met jullie
allemaal, van mij mag je natuurlijk niets denken.
Ik denk zo vaak aan jou. Hoe gaat het met Lies
Gis ze er nog. Van Lies heb ik door mevrouw Gies
gehoord, dat ze nog hier is. Wij zijn zelven onbekend,
en hebben ge zelschap, verder mag ik over ons
leven niets schrijven, hoewel het erg maar interes-
sant voor later is. Te lang mag de brief niet
worden dus tot ziens en een klein kusje van Anne

Beste Pop,   25 Sept. 1942.

The farewell letters from Anne to Jacqueline.

wenst je

Anne Frank

Aan
Mej. J. N. Maarsen
Amsterdam
Hunzestraat 4

NEDERLAND
AMS   C.S.

Import

HNR SER 7006

Gelukkig Nieuw

A postcard from Anne to Jacqueline, January 1942.

Jacqueline.v.Maarsen wordt uitgeno-

digd opZondag. ﹖. Maart bij Anne

Frank, Merwedeplein 37, te 11 uur,

voor een filmvoorstelling.

&&& &&& &&& &&&

MRT 1942

Z.O.Z.

Zonder deze kaart geen toegang.

Z.O.Z.

Wanneer men verhinderd is te komen,

gelieve tijdig te waarschuwen.

tel.90441

MRT 1942

rij II plaats 2.

An invitation made by Jacqueline and Anne to one of their parties.

Jacqueline's parents, circa 1925.

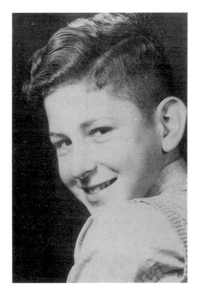

Ruud in 1943.

Jacqueline (front right) with her cousins: Meta (sitting on the swing), Betsy (standing on the swing), and Deetje (behind Jacqueline). (Jacqueline's sister, Christiane, is standing front left.) Summer 1940.

Otto Frank with Jacqueline in 1970.

never found out about it, and the problem of the "white lie" went away.

It took until October 1943 before my father was permitted to remove the yellow star from his coat. That had to do with the sterilization of Jews with "Aryan" spouses to prevent Jews married to non-Jews from reproducing. Some doctors evaded this law by issuing false statements of sterilization. My father somehow managed to get a copy of one of these statements.

After that, there were no more Jews to be seen in the city. By then they had all been removed or had gone into hiding. All of my Jewish uncles, aunts, and cousins were gone, as well as my father's oldest brother. Although he was also married to a non-Jew, he had been picked up for breaking one of the ordinances.

During the previous months we had regularly seen long lines of Jews walking through the streets with their backpacks and bags, the German soldiers all around them with their guns pointed at them. Anyone who walked away was shot. One could hear the Germans shouting commands all through the quiet street—it always happened in the evening and late at night when other people were inside. It was not a good idea to go and stand by the window, since that infuriated the Germans. However, I took cover and looked anyway.

My father was called up by the Germans. His suitcase stood ready and waiting in the hall, but his departure date was continually postponed until the moment that he was able to remove his star. Thus my mother's actions saved my father's life as well.

Ruud

Children often played in the street in the neighborhood where the Hunzestraat and the Lekstraat met. The girls played hopscotch and marbles and jumped rope. The boys usually played on the vacant lot nearby. They built forts, and the older boys played soccer.

I didn't associate with the boys on my street, but one day I noticed that two of them stood out from the rest: they had yellow stars on their jackets. After a time they suddenly disappeared.

I saw one of the boys again on May 5, 1945. It turned out that he and his parents had been in hiding for about two years in an attic room at a neighbor's house. The other boy, Ruud—he would later become my husband—came back to live in the neighborhood several months after the war. He had also gone into hiding.

His parents had been hesitant about going into hiding. With the help of their doctor, Ruud's father was successful in outwitting the Germans during the raids so that their deportation could continue being postponed. As soon as they heard the Germans banging on the door, they tapped on the radiator. The neighbors heard it and telephoned the doctor, who lived in the Lekstraat and who came over immediately. The doctor then told the Germans that the man at the address had a serious, contagious disease. Ruud's father lay in bed with wet washcloths on his forehead, breathing heavily and rolling his eyes, playing the part of someone gravely ill. Muttering, "This will take care of itself, " the Germans quickly left. After this ploy had worked a couple of times, the Germans turned their attention to Ruud, saying that they would take the boy instead. At that point a miracle occurred when they took pity on my then future mother-in-law, who fell to her knees and begged them not to take her son: they left Ruud behind. At this point Ruud's parents realized that they had to get away at once.

A neighbor woman, who had been sheltering the other boy without the knowledge of anyone in the neighborhood, accompanied mother and son—naturally, without the yellow stars on their coats—on the train to the eastern part of Holland, risking inspection and immediate deportation. The father stayed in the neighborhood of Amsterdam. He looked too Jewish to go along on the train. His story: a lot of money paid, an unheated attic room, a bowl of soup that froze, an asthma patient and unable to cough for fear that the neighbors might hear. He died three years after the war.

Mother and son fared much better. An underground movement had been established in Twente that concerned itself with helping Jews go into hiding. A clergyman was the coordinator. They spent the first night with him. The next day they heard to their horror that they would not be staying together and were not allowed to know each other's addresses. The mother ended up with people in Enschede who took her in lovingly and full of understanding in spite of the danger into which they put themselves. The son ended up with a family in Nijverdal as the so-called nephew of the man of the house. The man worked for the town clerk and later even managed to have him registered as his son so that no problems would arise in the event of inspection.

The man's wife, Aunt Hilda, as I would later call her, had seen Jews at a remote train station being packed up and loaded for Germany. She was so upset by what she witnessed that when she got home, after discussing it with her husband, she went immediately to the local clergyman. She knew that he was in the Resistance and told him that she wanted to take in a Jewish child. Someone from the underground movement came to her with photographs of Jewish children from whom she could choose. She actually would have preferred a girl: that was easier, since

43

a girl could pose as a maid. When she heard that everyone wanted to have a girl and that they were stuck with all the boys, she chose Ruud.

Ruud quickly picked up on the fact that Aunt Hilda's mother disapproved of the family's taking in a Jewish boy. She saw the potential danger to the family with two small children and did not want her daughter to expose herself to it. This made Ruud feel insecure, and it gave him, especially in the beginning, a feeling of being unsafe. Later he understood that these people would stand behind him at all costs and that their trust in God was the guiding principle behind their doing what they felt had to be done.

Ruud went to visit his mother twice. (His mother's address was kept a secret.) Aunt Hilda accompanied him on the train. By then it had been more than a year since he had seen his mother. It was difficult. They had grown apart somewhat. Ruud had been under the influence of a family that was completely different from his own: in order not to arouse any suspicions he had to go with them to church, and the Bible was read daily. By the time Ruud and his mother had to say good-bye they had gotten reacquainted again, and that made parting difficult.

Ruud was not able to go to school and followed correspondence courses. However, he still enjoyed a relative amount of freedom. The area was sparsely populated, and he took walks in the woods, where one didn't encounter too many people. Sometimes he walked with a boy who had also come from western Holland; he was staying with his uncle temporarily because his mother was ill. At this uncle's house there were also two children, a brother and a sister. Although both Ruud and Gerrit knew that these children were Jewish, they never talked about it. Gerrit also knew full well why Ruud was in Nijverdal. He was only thirteen years old but never even hinted during the war that he knew. After the war he said, "I understood it from the very first day."

44

When the war was over, the farewells were heart-wrenching. Uncle Henk—Aunt Hilda's husband—took Ruud on a bicycle with only the rims of the tires remaining to his mother in Enschede, where they were reunited with his father after western Holland was liberated.

The Final War Years

During my "Jewish war years," until 1943, the world around me grew steadily smaller. We moved within a very small circle of people who were completely dependent upon each other due to the lack of interaction initiated by the outside world. There were so many places we couldn't go, and certainly nowhere outside Amsterdam, so that we children stayed strictly in the neighborhood of our own homes.

After that my horizons widened a bit. I went to other parts of Amsterdam and played hockey and tennis.

As I walked to school one day in July I thought about Anne. I was a bit lonely then and hadn't yet found my niche at Girls High School. I realized that she had been gone exactly one year to the day and missed her. A year later, in 1944, I recalled the day again and thought about the moment she would return from Switzerland and we would pick up our old friendship again where we had left off. Although by now I had made various new friends, I still looked forward to Anne's return. Many years later I got around to telling her father this. He was pleasantly surprised about it. He was an extrovert, just like his daughter Anne, and I was still as reserved as ever. Since I seldom talked about it, there was no way for him to know that I had been so preoccupied with her after she left. He then let me read Anne's first little plaid diary, which he kept in a safe in Basel. I had never wanted to ask about it.

During the rest of the war my family lived for the reports that struggled to get through to us and which slowly but surely grew more optimistic as far as the fighting was concerned. The faster the war was over, the greater the chance that family and friends would return from Germany in one piece, or so we thought. What we still didn't know then and could not even begin to imagine was that most of the Jews taken to Sobibor, where the earliest deportations had gone, had been sent straight to the gas chambers upon arrival and had been dead for a long time.

As a precautionary measure the war and the Resistance were not discussed at school with the children. There were children in the class whose parents were known to be Nazi sympathizers. There was also a teacher whom we didn't trust. Some teachers carried out a kind of silent resistance by leaving textbooks prescribed from a propagandistic viewpoint (e.g., history) unopened. Our geography teacher was suspected of being a member of the Resistance, but no one discussed it openly. He was the one who made sure that there was warm soup for the children at the end of the "hunger winter" of 1944–1945. He was also the one who arrived at school extremely shaken the same morning that I passed the still-smoldering remains of two large houses at the corner of the Apollolaan and Beethovenstraat on my way to school. A German had been "liquidated" by the Resistance. In retaliation a large number of imprisoned Resistance members were picked up that morning from jail, brought to the Apollolaan, and shot at the same spot where the German had been killed. As a second retaliatory gesture, the houses were set on fire. The Germans left the bodies there for a few hours as an example. Our teacher had passed by there early that morning.

Every now and then there were raids to track down Jews in hiding. When betrayal was involved (a monetary reward was paid for every Jew turned in, and it soon became obvious to us that even those not sympathetic to the Nazi regime rather liked the idea), there usually wasn't enough time to escape, certainly not in Amsterdam. Twice a distant relative fled to our house in panic. He knew that he would be safe with us in the event of an emergency. I barely knew him and stood in a corner of the hall looking at him, at the frightened eyes of someone being hunted. I was frightened, too: the Germans were still in the neighborhood, the house searches not yet over. They could have stormed inside our house at any moment as well, but that never happened. When it was dark, our relative disappeared again in search of a new hiding place.

Our food rations grew smaller and smaller. Even with coupons we frequently stood in long lines outside the stores hoping to get a turn before everything was gone. Once the "hunger winter" of 1944–1945 began it became even more difficult to obtain food. We stood in line at the crack of dawn in front of the bakery, which just might have a sodden roll to sell, which we then had to make do with for a long time. One saw exhausted people sitting in shop doorways because they couldn't walk any farther; they often had swollen legs as a result of starvation edema. Leftovers from the kitchens of the German soldiers were earmarked for schoolchildren. We walked back and forth to the Roelof Hartplein to have meals at a school there. Sometimes it tasted good, sometimes even delicious (we weren't too picky anymore), but sometimes it turned out to be soup made from potato peels, which turned my stomach. Then there were the tulip bulbs and sugar beets, which the people of Amsterdam survived on in the end. With a lot of money or by walking for miles out to a farm one might be able to find some potatoes or beans. Things that were scarce, such as linens, soap, and matches, were good items to trade to farmers. The gas and electricity had been cut off, and we cooked on a little emergency burner that didn't require much fuel. It didn't warm the room either, and we went to bed early to avoid feeling the cold.

At one of my clubs I met a boy who fell in love with me. One evening he brought me home and went upstairs with me. It was the middle of the "hunger winter." We still had a bag of dried beans, and my mother would cook a smidgen of them a couple of times a week. During that period one of Deetje's father's cousins frequently came to our house after dark with her husband. They would warm themselves a bit at the burner that had been lit to cook the beans and would eat with us afterward. They were starving. There was no food left at the home in which they were hiding, and they had no money. I saw them sneak a bean out of the pan now and then. After we finished eating they would leave again and return to an address unknown to us.

When I got upstairs that evening with Thijs, he looked at the semidark corner where they sat and asked softly, "Are those Jews?" Startled, I thought about the "white lie" and said, "No." It was obvious that he didn't believe me when I denied it. I don't know whether they heard it. I never mentioned it, but our dinner guests never returned after that. Thijs didn't either. He said that he didn't want to associate with Jews.

It was April 1945. The liberation of western Holland was close at hand, but the hunger in the cities was so pervasive that the longer liberation took, the more people died. The food supply had been exhausted. The Allies decided to drop packages of food over Amsterdam.

We were sitting in class when we heard the airplanes fly over. The whole school ran up to the roof. We waved our shawls and handkerchiefs at those pilots from the free world, our friends, and gazed at the falling cloud of black specks.

On the other side of the water there was a large house where German officers were quartered. We saw them watching us through the windows. After witnessing our elation for a while, they stormed over to our school principal and ordered that we come down from the roof.

The bakers baked bread from the flour that dropped out of the sky and landed in a pasture. Never again have I tasted bread as good as the "Swedish white bread," smeared with margarine that had fallen from the sky with the flour.

May 1945—Mr. Frank

The happiness I felt the morning I awakened after Germany surrendered would not be dampened by memories of all of my war experiences. I didn't want to dwell on them for the time being.

There was a strange transition period the first few days. One individual who had not turned in his radio set it on the windowsill, and people swarmed around to listen to the good news. The Canadians who had liberated us in Amsterdam (we would immediately learn the Canadian national anthem at school) were advancing, and the Germans had not yet departed. Suddenly a group of German soldiers appeared. Silently they pointed their rifles at the crowd of people listening to the radio. In panic we tried to run away, with everyone treading on top of each other. They didn't shoot at us, though. Their silence lent something unreal to the situation. We heard later that shots had been fired at the Dam Square near the Royal Palace. One girl from my hockey club, who had joined in the frantic rejoicing taking place on the square, was shot along with a few others from the building that had been occupied by German officers during the war, and where they now sat awaiting what was to come.

Then there was a succession of unusual events. We were walking around in our old, worn-out clothes and still had nothing to eat, but that no longer bothered us. The whole war had been gray and drab. Now everything looked sunny and clear to me again. We waited for the Canadians by the Berlagebrug and rode with them to the Vondelpark, where they pitched their tents and handed out cans of food, chocolate, and cigarettes. Since there was no public transportation we had to walk the whole way back, but we didn't care. On the way back we ate the chocolate, which we hadn't tasted in such a long time.

Then the street parties began. Committees were established in every neighborhood to organize all kinds of events. We went from one street party to the next with our friends and danced until the middle of the night to American music.

The action of liberation frenzy was followed by an equal and opposite reaction. The supply of food gradually got under way, but at the same time the first reports trickled down about the concentration camps and the condition of the survivors when the Allies arrived to liberate them. What we could hardly believe during the war turned out to be true. Until I saw the first photographs and films that were made when the camps were liberated, there was no way I could even imagine it.

The daughter of one of my father's friends returned from Auschwitz and came straight to us. At that moment she knew no one else in Amsterdam. It turned out later that her father, her mother, and practically the rest of her family would never be coming back. She fell into my mother's arms, sobbing. Her concentration camp number had been tattooed on her arm. That night she described to my parents all of the horrors she had experienced. I was sent to bed. She was only a year older than I was.

We waited to hear whether more family members or friends would be coming back, but it remained frighteningly quiet.

All of a sudden Anne's father was standing in front of our door. He was alone; I didn't understand. I didn't understand the sad eyes on his sunken face either until he told us his story and the terrible truth hit us: that he had gone into hiding behind his office on the Prinsengracht with the van Pels family and Mr. Pfeffer, the dentist,* and that they had been betrayed and deported. Mr. Frank said that Anne had been happy in Wester-bork because she could feel the sun again and was able to move

*In *The Diary of a Young Girl:* the van Daan family and Mr. Dussel.

around more. He also told us that they had been put on the last transport to Poland and that the men and women had been separated almost immediately. He had been with Peter van Pels until the end at Auschwitz, but once the Allies were advancing Mr. Frank was left behind in the infirmary while Peter was forced to accompany the Germans, who withdrew from the camps, away from the Allies, in the direction of Germany. It turned out later that almost no one returned from these death marches. Peter didn't. Mr. Frank was liberated a couple of days later by the Russians.

By the time Mr. Frank arrived on our doorstep he had already heard that his wife, Edith, had died, but he had heard nothing about Margot and Anne and still hoped that they had survived the concentration camp. Lists arrived from the Red Cross. The whole war the Red Cross hadn't dwelled too much on the Jewish situation, but now they appeared with the lists neatly kept by the Germans of the Jews they had killed, where, and when. Those who had been in hiding or had survived the camps went regularly to read the lists, and so my father discovered little by little that no one from his family was ever coming back. Meta and Deetje were on one of the lists, too.

Mr. Frank continued to go and look at the lists, but in between he asked those who returned from the camps whether they knew anything about his daughters. As a result, before Margot's and Anne's names even appeared on the list, he came across a nurse who had been there with her sister when first Margot and, the next day, Anne died.

He cried and cried. He came to see me often, and I was at a loss as to how to console him. The only thing I could do was talk to him about his children, and that was really the only thing he wanted. At that time he lived with Miep and Jan Gies, who had lived across from us on the Hunzestraat during the war. He told us about the role that Miep had fulfilled, taking care of eight people in hiding on the Prinsengracht. We had watched her come and go throughout the entire war and knew that she worked at Mr. Frank's office, but had never associated her with the disappearance of the Frank family. The letter that had been left behind at Merwedeplein, about Switzerland, had worked. I suddenly understood where the chairs from the house at Merwedeplein had gone.

Mr. Frank also visited Jetteke often then. Jetteke had been Margot's best friend since Girls High School, and they were in the same class later at Jewish High School, where they were part of a close-knit group together with another girl named Trees and her boyfriend, Bram—both classmates.

This evening Margot and I talked about Bram and Trees in the bathroom! (March 23, 1944)

Bram, Trees, and Jetteke had survived the war. It was Jetteke whom Mr. Frank wanted to talk to about Margot. Both of his daughters had been equally dear to him. The fact that he concentrated more on Anne later was due to the diary that Anne kept from her birthday on June 12, 1942, until the day that they were deported, on August 4, 1944. Miep had found Anne's completely filled pages and her first little plaid diary in the abandoned annex on the Prinsengracht and had saved everything to give to Anne when she returned. When Miep knew for sure that Anne was dead, she turned everything over to Mr. Frank, unread.

Anne's Diary

After Mr. Frank had read Anne's writings, he came to our house. He had brought along one of the large gray cash books filled with her writings that had been found. I looked at it briefly but didn't read it. I saw that Anne's handwriting had improved over the years. Anne always wrote with her pen between her index finger and her middle finger because she had sprained her thumb at some point. I had always admired her handwriting and tried to imitate it by holding my pen the same way. I had an irregular, slanted handwriting style, and holding my pen the way she did enabled me to write straight up and down; this improved my penmanship, but my handwriting ended up looking different from Anne's. I continued holding my pen straight up and down between those two fingers for years, thinking of her often as a result.

Mr. Frank mentioned some time later that he had been advised to have the diary published. He knew that Anne had thought about publishing the diary herself: at a certain point she had started rewriting it from the beginning, omitting what she considered inappropriate for publication. Miep had been able to save both versions. In the second version, my name had been changed to *Jopie*. At first I thought that Anne's father had done that, but he told me that she had invented the name herself.

For years I was able to hide behind that name. No one knew that I had been Anne's best friend, and as far as I was concerned, it could stay that way. When my daughter was twelve, she asked me whether she could finally tell her girlfriend that her mother was the Jopie in the diary. Sometimes my husband would suddenly raise the topic as well, and a look from me wasn't always enough to silence him. In addition, I didn't like the name Jopie. It would be years before I figured out how she came up with that name, as well as the name Kitty. A girl by that name lived at Merwedeplein. I didn't know her well, but I knew that Anne used to play outside with her and liked her. Mr. Frank and I discussed once whether it might have been that Kitty to whom Anne addressed the entries in her diary. I believe that he even talked to Kitty about it. It remained unclear, and we didn't think the puzzle would ever be solved.

And then I made a discovery while reading *The Diary of Anne Frank: The Critical Edition*. At the bottom of the page containing the two letters that Anne had written to me, yet another letter had been printed:

Dearest Pop:
Just a short scribble, you haven't heard from me for a long time have you, but things are still all right. How is Kees? When will it be, he is a really good boy friend isn't he, but I don't really have to ask you, since you obviously think that anyway of your intended. (September 25, 1942)

Until then Anne's original manuscripts had been read primarily by men, or by women who had not grown up speaking Dutch. They didn't know who Pop and Kees were. I did know. Pop was one of Joop ter Heul's friends and belonged to the original "Jopopinoloukico Club," a name derived from a combination of the names of the girls in the book (Joop, Pop, Pien, Noor, Louk, Kitty, and Connie). Kees was Joop ter Heul's brother and was going steady with Pop. Anne also addressed some of her letters to Connie and Pien, but primarily to Kitty. Kitty was a perky, easygoing girl. She was Joop's best friend. Anne identified with her the most. Suddenly I knew why Anne had called me Jopie: after Joop ter Heul, by Cissy van Marxveldt. I read this sentence in Anne's diary:

As you've never been through a war, Kitty . . . (July, 1943)

No, the Kitty from *Joop ter Heul* had certainly never been through a war.

I dug through an old box for my one remaining part of the Joop ter Heul series. I had saved it because it had been signed by Cissy van Marxveldt. She was married to one of my father's cousins, which is how I ended up with a signed copy. I started reading it. It no longer captivated me, but it suddenly dawned on me that the first part of Anne's diary had been written in the style of the then often-read book.

Otto Frank decided to have the diary published for two reasons: first, to pay homage to his dead daughter, and second, because he knew that was what she would have wanted. He put together a version that contained the first part that had been rewritten by Anne herself (she had not yet finished it in August 1944), followed by the last part, which she had not rewritten. He omitted certain passages he considered uninteresting or derogatory toward his late wife.

He gave me copies of two letters that Anne had addressed to me in her diary. The first one was the promised "farewell letter" I had searched for in the abandoned house at Merwedeplein. These letters had been dated September 1942. After reading the first letter I realized that she must have written it to me shortly after going into hiding: "when you telephoned me on Sunday afternoon," or perhaps even earlier: "I must leave." Nothing would have been easier than for Miep to drop it in the mailbox to me, but then I would have figured out that Anne was still in Amsterdam and the rumor about Switzerland had to remain intact. I think that she must have rewritten this letter to me in her diary in September. In her second letter, she thanked me for my reply. However, I had never answered her. I had never received her letter and throughout the whole war assumed that she was safe in Switzerland. She made up a reply from me and answered the fictitious letter. Presumably, the original letter was lost or discarded by Anne herself.

<u>This is the promised fare-well letter:</u>

September 25, 1942

Dear Jacqueline,

I am writing this letter in order to bid you good-by, that will probably surprise you, but fate has decreed that I must leave (as you will of course have heard a long time ago) with my family, for reasons you will know.

When you telephoned me on Sunday afternoon I couldn't say anything, for my mother had told me not to, the whole house was upside down and the front door was locked. Hello was due to come, but we didn't answer the door. I can't write to everyone and that's why I'm writing to you. I'm taking it that you won't talk to anybody about this letter nor from whom you got it. I would be so grateful if you would be really nice and keep up a secret correspondence with me. <u>All inquiries to Mrs. Gies!!!!</u> I hope we'll meet again soon, but it probably won't be before the end of the war. If Lies or anyone else asks you if you've heard anything from me say absolutely nothing, otherwise you'll get us and Mrs. Gies into mortal trouble, so I hope you'll be really careful. Later, of course, you'll be able to tell people that you had a farewell letter from me. Well then Jackie, I hope things go well with you, that I hear from you soon and that we'll meet again soon.

Your <u>"best"</u> friend <u>Anne</u>

P.S. I hope that we'll always stay <u>"best"</u> friends until we meet again.

<u>'bye</u>

The second letter:

September 25, 1942

Dear Jackie,
    I was very glad to get your letter, if no Germans have been to our apartment so far, please could you go round to Mr. Goldschmidt and pick up some of our books and papers and games you can have them or look after them for me, or else you could take them to Mrs. Gies. I forgot to tell you in my last letter that you must not keep these letters from me, because <u>no one must</u> find them. So cut them up into tiny pieces, just like we did that time on the terrace with the letter from Mummy's box. Please do it. How are you all, I mustn't write about myself of course. I think of you so often. How is Ilse is she still around. I've heard from Mrs. Gies that Lies is still here. We're not bored and we have company, I mustn't write anything more about our life until later, although it is weird but interesting. This letter mustn't get too long be seeing you and a little kiss from

<u>Anne</u>

    I will now immediately reveal the mystery of the "letter from Mummy's box." I once heard the slightly sneering remark, "The two of you read dirty letters," and I noticed in the English version of Anne's diary that the Dutch word *briefje* had been translated as "letter."* It was a box of tampons, and the letter in question was the directions for use.

*Anne uses the Dutch word *briefje* to describe printed paper, which is not uncommon in the Dutch language; however, as a result, some confusion arose as to the meaning of the word.

Het Achterhuis

The first publishing house that Mr. Frank approached was not interested in Anne's manuscripts. They just couldn't see it and were afraid that it would be a money-losing proposition. I certainly understood that at the time: why would anyone be interested in the confessions of such a young child? And who wanted to hear anything more about the war at that point? When Mr. Frank finally succeeded in finding a publisher and came to me, at the publisher's request, to ask me if I would write something about our friendship, I declined for the very same reasons. He invited me to have lunch with him in the Kalverstraat, where he broached the subject. I told him that I could not imagine anyone being interested in the fact that Anne had read *Joop ter Heul* with her best friend, played Monopoly, or collected pictures of movie stars. In addition, I wouldn't even think of divulging that sex was one of Anne's favorite subjects to discuss whenever we were together. There was no way I could have known that those who had studied Anne's complete writings had been aware of that for a while, nor could I have known that my name had been mentioned numerous times in connection with this topic.

Or only spoke on the subject when I was alone with Jacque . . . (January 24, 1944)

I also didn't know then that Anne had described the scene about feeling each other's breasts and that her father had read it, too. I think that he did show it to my mother then, in light of one of the statements she made during an interview that she gave in 1956.

Many years went by before I could read *Het Achterhuis* objectively and understand why it struck such a responsive chord in people around the world. It was not until 1970 that it finally sank in, when Mr. Frank brought me a book containing letters that he had received over the years from people who had read his daughter's diary. It was then that I realized how the diary worked. Apart from Anne's character, which appealed to so many people, there was also the fact that this young girl who still expected so much out of life had been killed in such a fashion. People were able to relate to that much easier than to the figure of six million dead Jews.

Whenever anything by or about Anne was published, her father brought me a copy of it. He subsequently gave me foreign editions of her book when I visited him in Basel. More copies of Anne's book have been sold than of any other book in the entire world except the Bible. I have about fifty editions in my bookcase, published in many countries in many languages.

When I received the first edition of Anne's diary from her father in 1947, I had the feeling that I was reading something that was not meant for me to read. I did not look at it again for many years and never told anyone that I had known Anne. Once I overcame that hurdle, another reason arose as to why I did not want to talk about my friendship with Anne. In the United States a play had been written after the book, and then a movie was made, and the book became world-famous. Suddenly there were people who prided themselves on having known Anne or been friends with her. Strangely enough, those were never her real acquaintances or friends, but people who had never even known her or noticed her; they had been in a different class at school or hadn't played with her because they had associated with a different group of children. I have always been very reticent about this subject because I didn't want to become important because of a girlfriend who perished in a concentration camp.

In 1953 Anne's father remarried and he moved to Basel.

From there he would travel all over the world to meet people who were interested in Anne's diary and in the persecution of the Jews by the Nazis. Otto Frank was received by the most important people in the world.

He died in 1980 at the age of ninety-one. He had devoted his life after the war to his daughter's writings. He answered letters from children and adults who had read Anne's diary and wanted to convey their feelings to him about it. He also opened schools that were named after her. Statues and memorial stones of and for Anne were unveiled in his presence.

Once the proceeds from the sale of Anne's book began pouring in, Otto Frank established a foundation: the Anne Frank Foundation. The purpose of the foundation was to combat discrimination, using the persecution of the Jews as an example—for which Anne served as a symbol—and to further Anne's ideals as they were left to the world in her diary. The money was also to be given to charitable causes with more or less the same purpose. The house on the Prinsengracht where the eight people described by Anne had gone into hiding became the foundation headquarters and was turned into a museum.

Mr. Frank stayed extremely busy with all of this. Whenever he was in Amsterdam for meetings, he phoned. The foundation and people involved with it kept him so busy that he often had no time to come and visit. Many of his earlier acquaintances started making great demands on his time as well. Whenever we saw each other he usually brought me a small gift, and I received the same warm affection from him that his daughter had extended to me and with the same effusiveness that always embarrassed me.

In the beginning I didn't want to ask him to let me see the house where they had remained in hiding. In the meantime it had been named the Anne Frank House and in later years would become the most frequently visited museum in Amsterdam. However, at some point he took me and showed me the rooms where Anne had spent those years. It made quite an impression on me, being there with Anne's father, who had so many sad memories of the house.

Then I saw the wall that Anne had plastered with pictures of movie stars and postcards. This was something that belonged to the two of us. We had busied ourselves with these movie stars together. Among the postcards on the wall were two of the English princesses, Elizabeth and Margaret Rose. *Did she have those, too?* I wondered. My sister and I had received a series of four cards of the British royal family when we were in Paris in 1938 while the king and queen of England were visiting. I didn't give it any more thought.

However, one day I suddenly came across a Shirley Temple card that was addressed to Margot Frank. Then I realized what must have happened. I had given my two cards of the princesses to Anne in exchange for her Shirley Temple card. I quickly leafed through my postcard collection. I found what I was looking for: the two remaining postcards from the series of four. The other two are hanging on the wall in the Anne Frank House.

Mr. Frank and I wrote to each other regularly. I received cards from him from all over the world. When my husband and I traveled with our children to France, we would always stop by and see him in Basel.

One time, when we were on our way to Basel again, I realized that our older son had never read *Het Achterhuis*. I had to urge him to do so because I knew that Mr. Frank enjoyed talking to children about his daughter. I sensed in my own children the same embarrassment I always felt upon reading the diary, particularly in my younger son, who is a lot like me.

In 1952 I was in England, living with a couple in London, taking care of their three-year-old daughter. The mother was an author of children's books, and the father was an editor for the *New Statesman*. One day he came home with a book that had been received by the editorial staff and said to me, "This was written by a Dutch girl; you might find it interesting reading." I looked at it and thought, *I know that girl.* It was *The Diary of a Young Girl,* by Anne Frank, the first English edition. I had read Anne's diary five years earlier, and now I read it again for the second time, in English. For the first time, however, I read that Anne had described the incident about the breasts in complete detail. It said "a friend," but I still remembered the incident well. At that point it dawned on me that Anne's father had omitted it from the Dutch version, and I was thankful to him for that. He told me later that it had been the Dutch publisher who felt that it should not be published. (That was in 1947.) However, Mr. Frank had extracted my name from the manuscripts from which *Het Achterhuis* had been published. As shocked as I was when I read it, I was still very touched that Anne had written in all honesty in her diary: "She refused."

When my host gave me the book, I didn't tell him that I was Jopie, and after reading it I pondered whether to do so. A friend of the woman of the house was staying with them, and since we sat reading together in front of the fireplace, I asked her as soon as I had finished the book whether she wanted to read it. She looked at it disparagingly with her lips drawn into a thin line and said no. I never told my story. It was my oversensitivity to anti-Semitism—acquired during the war—getting the better of me then.

When the war ended I was sixteen years old. I wanted to start afresh and forget those preceding dark years to the extent possible. For my father that was impossible. His whole family had been massacred. It was true that anti-Semitism had been officially renounced, but it had also been fanned by the war, and that was still palpable afterward. My sister and I did not have the slightest desire to become Jewish again. Thus there was my father with two non-Jewish daughters at precisely the time that he had become devout and sought solace in the synagogue. His relationship with my mother had not been helped by the difficult war years. He never really got over these times but developed a heart ailment and died in 1952.

Anne Frank

In 1952 *Het Achterhuis* appeared in the United States. A play was also produced under the supervision of Otto Frank. And a movie was made. Milly Perkins played Anne. In 1956 the Dutch-language version of the play appeared. There were some small changes introduced. In order to give the whole play an extra dramatic touch, Otto appeared onstage at the beginning, portraying the moment when he saw the secret annex for the first time after the war. He finds Anne's diary lying on the floor and a shawl that Anne had knitted for him from scraps of wool. I thought that was a good beginning. Jetteke and I were both invited to the premiere by Mr. Frank. "Jopie" was also mentioned in the play. Ruud and I looked at each other. No one knew that I was that Jopie. It was a strange sensation for me. I thought that it was an impressive performance, but it was not Anne standing there on the stage, no matter how well it was played. Queen Juliana also attended the premiere. Mr. Frank never wanted to see the play.

I saved the playbill. It was the beginning of my collection of mementos and newspaper clippings from the journey that my friend's diary would make starting at that moment.

At that point people started getting curious about Anne's background. People who had known her were being interviewed. During the first two years of our marriage, Ruud and I lived in Brussels, where our daughter was born, and in the fall of 1956 we returned to Amsterdam.

Someone wanted to write a book about Anne that would include interviews of people who had known her well. Because we had just moved back from Brussels, our telephone hadn't yet been connected, and the man stopped by our house one evening without having made an appointment. We weren't there that evening, and my mother was taking care of our little girl. When we returned home my mother told us about the man's visit. She had told him that she still remembered everything about Anne very clearly and, in fact, probably remembered her better than I did. I thought it was a strange remark and wondered what she could have told him. She had never paid much attention to my friends and had little patience for children's stories. Anyway, I was glad that I had managed to get out of the interview and left it at that.

However, when I read the interview of my mother in the book, I was both surprised and disappointed. *Where in the world did she get that?* I thought when I read it. I discovered that as soon as my mother had seen Anne's diary displayed in all of the store windows, she suddenly remembered all sorts of things about my friendship with Anne.

It wasn't completely made up. The story about Anne's having put her cat in the bath was true. And she indeed showed my mother her new blue dress, because she knew that my mother was interested in clothing. Anne had just come from the seamstress, and I can still see her standing in the room, showing off her dress. However, what wasn't in the book was that Anne primarily wanted to show my mother the ingenious way in which the skirt had been invisibly lengthened. I have heard my mother tell an embellished version of this story so many times. The book said that my mother made the dress. That must have been a misunderstanding, probably due to the fact that my mother spoke French and the interviewer German.

That was the first time I encountered the phenomenon of someone trying to make herself appear important by telling stories about Anne. More and more often after that I heard people saying—sometimes through the grapevine and sometimes firsthand—that they had known Anne, played with her, or been in the same class with her at school. There were even acquaintances of mine who mentioned it in my presence when both of us knew full well that it wasn't true. In the beginning I would challenge such remarks, saying, "How is that possible?" and, "But you were . . . " Later I just kept my mouth shut. I didn't think it was right to prove them to be liars in front of their spouses or friends. It surprised me that someone would attribute status to being a friend of Anne Frank's, but I left it at that. It didn't concern me personally, even though it was annoying that these remarks were being validated by my silence; however, I had no solution. I didn't want to initiate a conflict over this sensitive subject.

One time the opposite occurred. It was during the late sixties. One of my distant cousins went to live and work in Eindhoven. She became friends with someone who told her that he had gone to school with Anne Frank. She told him that one of her cousins had also been a classmate of Anne's at Jewish High School. He couldn't remember my name and didn't trust the story, as he had experienced this same phenomenon on several different occasions. When my cousin told me his name, I recognized it immediately. He was the boy who had been sexually enlightened by Anne. I told her, "Tell him I still remember that he sat next to Leo S. in class." I was right and he believed me. Later on I ran into him on a regular basis and together we would resurrect old memories of those days.

I generally didn't talk too much about the war and certainly not about Anne. I had a busy life with a family of three children, to whom I devoted myself completely. I was glad that Anne's father kept me informed as to everything that was happening in connection with Anne's diary. I followed its rise with interest. Whenever there were commemorations or unveilings related to Anne, her father included me. Miep Gies and her husband were always present as well. The ceremonies usually took place in the Anne Frank House.

Famous

June 12, 1979, I sat in the Westerkerk (a church in the center of Amsterdam near the Anne Frank House) with a large number of other invitees who had gathered to commemorate what would have been Anne's fiftieth birthday. There were various speakers, and appropriate songs were sung. My attention wandered and I looked at Anne's father. Had he gotten used to the fact by now that his daughter had become the symbol of the millions of Jews killed by the Nazis?

I could not see Anne as a symbol. To me she was still my little friend. I thought about her thirteenth birthday, thirty-seven years ago. With sparkling eyes she had watched her friends enter and opened her presents expectantly. She had enjoyed being the center of attention and continued to enjoy it after everyone had left, while we organized her gifts. I still remember that so well because I didn't see her diary lying there, which surprised me, since it was her most important present. She would never know how important it would become.

> One way or another everyone will know my name later [she wrote in the story "Movie Star Illusions" on December 24, 1943].

Now I sat there listening quietly; everyone knew her name and talked about her, but for that she had had to die first. We didn't think about dying that day in June 1942; our lives had just begun.

On the occasion of this commemoration I wanted to do something for Mr. Frank as a token of my friendship with him and with his daughter. My children had grown up in the meantime, and I had been studying book binding for several years. I had chosen this profession because it enabled me to combine my love of literature, love of books as objects, and love of artistic handicraft. When I was no longer able to further my knowledge in Holland, I traveled to Paris every six months to take lessons there. I had planned for *Het Achterhuis* to be the first book that I would bind in leather without the help of my teacher.

At the Westerkerk, I presented it to Mr. Frank. He was pleased with it and, as a favor to me, showed it immediately to a publisher friend.

I made a binding for *Het Achterhuis* twice more after that. I had a second copy of the first edition and made a binding in the style of the period in which the book was written, with a gilt floral wreath on the front cover. The second time I made the binding for a book-binding contest. I used a French edition and applied the same decoration to the front cover that I had used on the book for Mr. Frank. On the back cover I expressed my deepest feelings. I received an honorable mention, and the book was purchased by the Royal Library in The Hague. I concealed the fact that I was the Jopie who appeared in the book. Later I discussed it with a friend who felt, as a historian, that my having been Anne's friend would add an extra dimension to the copy of the book I had bound, and he advised me to come out in the open with it. That made sense to me, and later, when I met the curator of book bindings, I told him. When my binding was displayed at the next exhibition, I read in the exhibition catalog: "This binding . . . displays an intense relationship to its content." I had requested that the information not be made public and found this to be a good solution.

After the official ceremony in the Westerkerk ended, Mr. Frank came up to me and said, "I want to introduce you to someone. You were one of the first ones I came to after I knew that Anne was dead. This is the woman who was with Anne when she died and whom I told you about then." It was one of the B. sisters, who had been nurses at the concentration camp and had seen Anne and Margot die.

Many beautiful words were spoken that afternoon, but at that point I didn't know what to add. I was afraid that I wouldn't fit in if I expressed my personal feelings, and so I didn't. I confined myself to shaking her hand and giving her a friendly nod.

Anne's fiftieth birthday was an inducement for German television to make a documentary about her. At first, it seemed like a good idea to me to air a program in Germany about the Nazi period—at that time that seldom happened—and I agreed to their request to work with them on it. Second, Mr. Frank and Miep Gies were going to appear in the documentary, and although I wanted to avoid the publicity surrounding this subject as much as possible, I felt that I belonged there with them. The interviews were inserted in the documentary between film clips of the rehearsals for the play from *Het Achterhuis* as performed by German high school students. Suddenly a girl about eighteen years old said, referring to the persecution of the Jews, "Why didn't anyone tell us about this? Are our parents all liars?" I was satisfied that I had cooperated in making the documentary.

August 20, 1980, the radio was on and I heard on the news: "Otto Frank, the father of Anne Frank, the girl who wrote the now world-famous diary during the war, died at his home in Basel." It did not come as a shock. The previous month I had visited him in Basel while he lay sick in bed, and I had known that would be the last time that I would ever see him.

Ruud was out of town then. I couldn't see myself going alone by car or by train to Basel, but even so, I wanted to go. While still pondering the matter, I received a phone call from the Anne Frank Foundation. They had chartered an airplane, and fortunately, Miep Gies had remembered to include me in the list of people who would go and take part in the ceremony.

The group departed for Basel, and the ceremony was reported on in detail in all of the newspapers.

Afterward we went with Mrs. Frank to her house. I was standing in a corner observing the chatter that usually prevails at these kinds of occasions when she approached me with one of her Swiss acquaintances. She introduced me to her: "This is Jopie."

"Oh, the whole diary is here," the woman said, surprised.

"Only the ones who aren't dead," I answered, smiling politely.

Afterward Mrs. Frank told me she had a tape from Otto that she had planned to play, but she didn't want to spoil the mood. I said, "Otto is the reason for our getting together."

A little later we all listened to the voice of Mr. Frank. He told his life story, which he had told shortly before at a school in Basel. I had heard and read his biography many times before, but all at once it struck me how proudly he mentioned that he had been an officer in the German army. That was during World War I, thus before the Nazi period; but I could not understand it: this very same country had caused him so much pain. I have observed this phenomenon often among German Jews.

Involvement

It was May, 1982, and the Anne Frank Foundation had been in existence for twenty-five years. There was a gathering in the Anne Frank House, and once more I sat in the familiar hall listening to the speeches. I thought about how Anne would have loved it, all of this attention being devoted to her. Impulsively I mentioned this to one of the foundation's board members. She hadn't recognized me immediately, so I reminded her that we had walked to the Tinguely Fountain together in Basel two years earlier—whenever I'm in Basel I usually walk by it—and then she remembered who I was. However, she was put out by my remark about Anne and said, "We mustn't think only of Anne. There were so many children who perished." I didn't answer; I was familiar with this type of peevish reaction but thought, *Here in this house, on this afternoon, when Anne's name is constantly on everyone's lips, we ought to be allowed to dwell on the child Anne Frank for a moment.* Through her, the pain that was inflicted on so many children became tangible.

I saw Miep and Jan Gies standing up ahead. I was reminded of something Miep had told me once that I could not understand at the time: they regularly received rude letters from people who felt that they were receiving too much attention while the letter writers had also done so much good during the war. By coincidence, Miep had helped Anne Frank, and as a result, she had drawn a lot of attention. She had actually become a symbol herself, but no matter how modest she was about it, the letters kept coming.

One important event was the opening of the exhibition "Anne Frank in the World" in Amsterdam in 1985. The queen was also in attendance, and I was introduced to her along with the B. sisters.

Lin Jaldati, one of the sisters, recited an excerpt from her theater program titled, "For Anne Frank," in which she told about Anne's last hours. Afterward she sang Yiddish songs with her husband and children. I thought of how splendid Anne would have thought it was that because of *her* book I received an introduction to the queen.

During the summer of 1987 I would be thoroughly confronted with the past again. I was informed that a film crew from the United States would be coming to Holland to make a film that would include interviews of people who had known Anne. Because I was on vacation in Italy at the time they were in Europe, they came and interviewed me there. However, they still wanted to visit with me several places in Amsterdam that were connected to Anne. That took place a couple of weeks later.

For the first time I stood inside the house at Merwedeplein again. It was forty-five years later. I asked the woman living there whether she knew which bedroom had been Anne's. I couldn't imagine at that moment which one it might have been. We usually played in the living room, which I still remembered well. I also remembered the kitchen where Anne always stood making sandwiches after school at four o'clock and where she fed her cat, Moortje. The same kitchen cabinets were still there, although they were hidden from view by wooden panels on the outside. The woman showed me a small room off to the side. I nodded, but the room didn't ring a bell. When we walked outside again it suddenly hit me: it couldn't have been Anne's room, at least not during the time that I knew her. I envisioned it once more in front of me, that unmade bed of Anne's and the new shoes with the wood laminate soles in front of it the day that I had gone inside the Frank family's abandoned house, the day after they had disappeared. The bed had been standing against the wall to the right of the door. That arrangement wasn't possible in that small room; on that wall there wasn't enough space next to the door. Then I remembered again which room had been Anne's.

After that we went to the school in the Stadstimmertuinen, where the school is located on the left side of the street when starting at the Amstel and continuing on through the arch. We came to the school playground. Memories that I had always suppressed resurfaced: of a playground full of children that grew steadily empty over the course of the year. There had been too many changes made to the classrooms; they didn't say anything to me. The gymnasium had remained unchanged. I recounted the school year that I had spent with Anne there. Good memories resurfaced as well. Later we walked from my previous home on the Hunzestraat to Anne's house at Merwedeplein. I showed the Hebrew letters on top of the gable of the synagogue on Lekstraat, which had stood there throughout the entire war, overlooked by the Germans. I had gazed at the letters often back then: a silent testimony to the prewar Jewish life there in the neighborhood that was then completely swept away.

On the Hunzestraat I pointed out Jan and Miep Gies's house and drew the film crew's attention to the bookstore on the corner where Anne's first little plaid diary had been purchased. I had figured out in the meantime what people wanted to hear, and like always, the film crew found all of the details extremely interesting.

They also wanted to go to the Oasis ice cream parlor, but there was no time left for that. Over the years I had gone there with people who wanted to retrace Anne's footsteps through the neighborhood. We would drink a cup of coffee there while my companion sat looking around, imagining that Anne had sat there, too. The situation was different, however. Not only had the interior been completely changed after the war, but we had also never sat inside there. The Jewish boys and girls from the neighborhood congregated there, but it was a social encounter played out on the sidewalk. One bought an ice cream and went outside to eat it. Sometimes we were treated to an ice cream:

> On Monday night I also met Mr. van Pels, who treated Jacque, Lies, Ilse and me to an ice cream, then we went to Oasis where we met Mr. Bernhardt, who also bought me an ice cream. (June 30, 1942)

I didn't know then that Mr. van Pels would later become "Mr. van Daan," the father of "Peter van Daan." To me he was one of Anne's father's vague acquaintances.

In the summer of 1943 no one was standing on the sidewalk in front of Oasis anymore.

While we were walking down the Lekstraat, I thought about a man whom I had encountered in the Bijenkorf department store two years earlier. At that time, forty years after the end of the war, many books were coming out about the war, and both of us stood there leafing through a book about the concentration camp Sobibor.

Suddenly he spoke to me. "My wife died there," he said. "We lived on the Lekstraat then, and she was taken away by the Germans. She was still so young. We had just married, right before the issuance of the racial decree that forbade mixed marriages. I even went to the Nazi Security Service on Euterpes-traat to plead with them to release her. I got into a fight there. I was kicked and beaten. They called me a *Judenfreund* [Jew-friend] as I stumbled out the door, bleeding. My shin was broken."

"Did you remarry later?" I asked him, curious. I was secretly hoping for a happy ending.

"No, I never married again," he answered. "I have never been able to forget her."

I laid my hand on the arm of this complete stranger, and we stood that way, looking each other in the eyes for a few seconds in the middle of the crowd of people in the book department of the Bijenkorf, into which we later disappeared, each in a different direction.

My Friend Anne Frank

In June 1989, on the occasion of the commemoration of Anne's sixtieth birthday, the exhibition "Anne Frank in the World" opened in New York, and the English translation of *The Diary of Anne Frank: The Critical Edition,* published by the Netherlands State Institute for War Documentation, came out in the United States. A few months later I was invited to go to Nevada to speak for two weeks to schoolchildren. The children had read Anne's diary and had learned about the Nazis from their teachers as a result of the exhibition, which had traveled in the meantime from New York to Nevada.

Years had gone by since Otto Frank's request that I tell about my memories of Anne. Meanwhile I had started writing my own diary. I wanted to record my perspective of what was happening in the world in memory of Anne. Now I considered the time ripe for telling my own story in a book, to write down everything as I had seen, heard, and experienced it. My book would be called *My Friend Anne Frank.**

I realized that going to Nevada would mean that I would be joining in the Anne Frank cult, which I had observed for years with mixed feelings. I knew that when I went to the United States I would let myself be seen, photographed, and entertained and that people would hang onto my every word as I told about my friendship with Anne Frank.

I thought about the little girl who had become "Anne Frank." I thought about the times that I am stopped on the street with the question: "Where is the Anne Frank House?," about my feelings when I see the name *Anne Frank* in newspaper

*Original Dutch title: "Anne en Jopie".

articles and when heads of state or other important people cite Anne Frank in their speeches.

In my book, the absurdity of this situation and the feeling of alienation it triggers in me could be illustrated by my experiences in Nevada. I reflected that it might be a good ending for my book and agreed to their request.

At the end of September I departed for the United States with Ruud. It was a tiring and interesting trip. I spoke to schoolchildren twice a day. I had prepared a lecture in which I described the Nazi period in general and my friendship with Anne in detail. For the remainder of the hour there was a question-and-answer period. I wasn't reserved anymore; they were allowed to ask me anything and everything. Even the incident about the breasts came up. When questions arose about going into hiding, I let Ruud tell his own story in order to give the children an idea of a different form of hiding during that time. It was a special experience for me to see how interested the children were in everything surrounding the war. By being there in person I brought a piece of history to life for them and lent authenticity to Anne's story. There were well thought out and funny questions. An Afro-American boy asked if the discrimination against the Jews was the same as the discrimination against Afro-Americans in the United States. Another wanted to know: "Why didn't you just fly away in an airplane?" Afterward children came to me for my autograph or to talk to me a little further. A small blond boy told me that his grandparents had been in Auschwitz and pointed to his arm, indicating that they had a number there. After the war they had moved to the United States, where his mother was born. At another school I met "Jopie," "Miep," "Margot," and "Peter." The children had performed the play the previous year. The girl who had played Jopie especially enjoyed having her picture taken with me. I liked that, too.

I was recognized and spoken to on the streets. Children and

teachers embraced me, sometimes with tears in their eyes. I experienced firsthand what an impression Anne's short life story had made upon them.

On a Friday evening I was to speak at the synagogue. I was listened to breathlessly, just as in the schools. It was an extraordinary experience for me, particularly since I dislike speaking in public. I was amazed at how easily it went.

We participated in a fund-raising lunch at the local Jewish Federation. It was interesting to see how that sort of thing was tackled: "Russian Jews are finally being allowed out of Russia, but we have to have money in order to take care of them." The governor of Nevada was also present, and I was introduced to him as Anne Frank's friend.

Once the "work" was done, Ruud and I were invited to parties, dinners, and shows; we were flown to the Grand Canyon in a private airplane.

Our visit was reported upon in the local newspapers and on television, and once we were filmed by the school television network: although we had visited twenty schools in ten days and had spoken to roughly three thousand children, there were still so many questions from schoolchildren not visited who would now be able to see us on film. After I had heard my speech numerous times it began to bore me. I longed for Amsterdam, for the silence of my book-binding atelier.

Twice, one of the teachers gave me a number of letters written to me by the children in the class I had visited. An excerpt from one of the letters follows: "Anne Frank is a very special person. That was cruel what they did. Hitler was a very bad person. It is hard to be without your best friend." She said that her grandmother was crazy about Anne Frank, and asked me to call her grandmother. She gave me the telephone number. "Tell her it's Anne Frank's best friend."

In the euphoria of that moment, a feeling that had come over me because of the events of the last few days, I thought when I returned to the hotel, *Let me call that woman and make her day.*

I walked to the telephone and started dialing the number, but all at once I thought about what I had heard one of the B. sisters say: "And then, then Anne was dead, too. We wrapped her in a blanket and laid her in the stinking mass grave . . . "

I wondered, *What am I doing? What am I going to say to this woman?*

I quietly put the receiver back on the hook.